Pain of Love

Erotic Poems by J.G. Frederick

Adult content. You have been warned.

Pain of Love

and all poems included
Copyright © 2012 I.G. Frederick

Second Edition

ISBN:
978-1-937471-97-2

Pussy Cat Press
http://pussycatpress.com/publisher.html/
P.O. Box 19764
Portland OR 97280

    All rights reserved. Except for use in review, the reproduction or utilization of this work in whole or in part in any form by any electronic, mechanical or other means now known or hereafter invented, is forbidden without the written permission of the author.

    Disclaimer: Names, characters, places and events described herein are products of the author's imagination or are used fictitiously and are not to be construed as real. Any resemblance to actual events, locations, organizations, or persons, living or dead, is entirely coincidental.

Acknowledgements

The Drummer appeared
on Oysters & Chocolate, May 25, 2010

The following poems have
previously appeared on
http://www.justusroux.com/:
"In Control" (December, 2009)
"Your Collar" (September, 2009)
"Heartfelt" (August, 2009)
"Lips" (August, 2008)
"Longing" (March 2007)
"The Party" (August 2006)
"Memories" (June 2006)
"The Gift" (February 2006)

Many thanks to those all those who have contributed to my success by sharing their knowledge, skills, and support, including Patrick, my boy, my love, my muse; Boy Robin, who served me well while he was under my protection; Cindy, my proofreader, editor and best friend and all those who inspired the poems herein.

Table of Contents

The Party 1

Heartfelt 2

Eruption 3

Your Collar 5

In Service 6

Switch 7

The Beast Within 8

In Control 9

The Gift 11

Leather Love 12

I'm Queer Too 13

Flying 15

Drummer 16

Breakable 17

Art Work 18

Fiction by I.G. Frederick 20

The Party

Leather slices through the air
slaps against flesh, marking it red.

Screams of pain echo through
the room, insulated from the

world outside with concrete
blocks and sound-proof tiles.

Black is the color of the night
but it comes in many shapes,

sizes, and configurations:
leather and lace, vinyl and rubber.

Bottoms' perverse pleasures
exceed tops' sadistic imaginations.

The smell of antiseptic competes
with the odor of burning candles

and sore arses compare whips to
floggers to snake tongues to paddles.

In the end, hugs, kisses, and caresses
ease the transition back to vanilla.

Heartfelt

So many have knelt
where you do now;
planted their lips on
my boots and thanked

me for the privilege.
None of it had
meaning. None of them
touched me. But when

you bow before me,
your heart bleeds through
your lips to bathe my
spirit with your

worship. When allowed
to look up, the
adoration in
your eyes fills me

with joy. You try to
express just how
grateful the honor
makes you and can't

comprehend that I
need you at my
feet as much as you
crave to serve me.

I.G. Frederick

Eruption

Your tongue leaves a trail
of molten lava
across my breasts while
I mark the heaving
mounds of your ass with
my lash. Our skin burns
with fire, consuming
all thoughts with the heat
of our lust. From the
depths, the eruptions
explode throughout our
bodies, changing the
landscape of our love.

Your Collar

You do not need the
collar to know that
you belong to me.
I fill your waking
thoughts and haunt your dreams.
You crave my touch, my
command, and the smile
that says you've pleased me.

I do not need to
put metal around
your neck to know that
I own you body
and soul. You prove it
every time you kiss
my feet or worship
my skin with your tongue.

Your collar bespeaks
the love we share, our
devotion to each
other. But I put
it there because I
need to claim you, to
tell the whole world that
you belong to me.

In Service

You tower over me,
but when I tug on your
hair you drop to your knees
and willingly submit
to my will.

I bite hard enough to
leave marks and you respond
with kisses. I whip your ass,
and you lick my neck, my
ear, my breasts.

When I ride your cock, you
give all pleasure to me,
waiting 'til I'm sated
before you request your
own release.

Switch

You say you're Dom
that others have
submitted to you.

And yet, you kneel
in front of me,
beg for my control.

I find you sweet,
soft, submissive,
pliant to my lash.

The challenge of
taking you down
is so very sweet.

The Beast Within

Come to me my incubus
my beast, my sweet adored one.

Ravish me, love me, wake the
succuba sleeping within.

Set my mouth, my skin aflame.
Ignite passion deep inside.

I will never get enough
of your touch to satisfy

the lifetime need you've caused to
rise. But my beast calls to yours

and together we will tear
apart the night with our cries.

In Control

If you peeked into my
bedroom, we'd not seem much
different than other
copulating couples:
bodies entwined, joined, skin
against silk. You'd have to
notice that my fingers
pull his hair hard; my teeth
mark his ear, shoulder, neck;
my nails etch red lines on
his back and chest. You must
listen closely to hear,
amidst the cries of his
pain and my pleasure, a
soft request for release.

The Gift

You kneel before me in supplication
offering your body and soul to my whim.
The sweat from your labor glistens
on pale skin striped with marks from my lash.

You rest your head on my foot and look up at me
with eyes that reveal every thought. I see the pain
mixed with pleasure; the intense need to serve;
and the hope that I will accept your gift.

The softness of your cheek on my foot soothes
away the tension in my soul. Your submission
fills a core need within me. Soon, my collar will
hang 'round your neck and bind you to me forever.

Leather Love

The sound of leather slapping against
flesh is an aphrodisiac that
makes me wet in anticipation
of your mouth on my lips. Your moans cause
my clit to reverberate against
your hot tongue. I bite into your flesh,
until my teeth leave marks. Tension builds
in my loins and I explode in your
face. You greedily lap up honey
until you sate your hunger. I grind
my hips into your face and tug on
your hair, pulling you closer as if
to swallow you into my pleasure.

I'm Queer Too

Outside, looking in.
Not into the "normal"
window. Not interested.

Outside of the Queer
community, left out
in the cold.

Yes, they stuck the
b in the middle.
But it may as well
stand for bitch.

The dykes take offense
at my mere presence.
I fuck men.
Not acceptable.

Doesn't matter that
I fuck women too.

I'm only welcome
if I never mention
male partners, if I
pretend I only
screw women.

Why? I respect their
right to limit themselves
to one gender. Don't
understand it, but
respect it.

I like women. Butch
or femme, dyke or bi.
Like men, too.

I'm pickier there.
Don't find bears
or sissies attractive.
Good friends, though.

Even in the leather
community, the
boys run off to play
by themselves.

The dykes have their own
group, too, although they're
more open to playing
with others.

Binary gender
options limit us so.
But, those hurt by
stereotypes have
prejudices of
their own.

Ditch them all!
If we think someone's
hot, we should have the
freedom to tell
her/him so without
worrying about
repercussions.

Flying

The lash of my whip
sent you flying through
the nightmares of your past.

I tried to hold you,
keep you from falling
into despairing depths.

But others in your
life can't understand
how you get high on pain.

They try to keep you
stranded on the ground,
barricaded from me.

I wish I could free
you from the prison
your mind has created.

I want to kiss you,
hold you, love you, but
I must watch from afar

as you stumble through
terror without the
release that pain can bring.

Drummer

Music pulses through the speakers,
fills the room with a techno beat.
Sticks, wooden spoons, pieces of pipe
beat out a staccato that will
leave bruises tomorrow morning.

The drummer dances to music
while she moves from ass to calves, from
feet to shoulders, from biceps to
thighs. The slap of wood and plastic
on skin keeps time with the primal

rhythm. The drum smiles serenely
processing the pain, feeling the
beat, sometimes tapping a toe or
fidgeting a finger. Mostly
he floats on an endorphin high.

Breakable

They crawl to us,
naked on their knees,
offering their skin
for us to mark
with our whips or canes.
We control the scene,

how they dress, act;
if they may speak.
We choose their
food and clothing;
whether they work
outside our homes.

But before we hang
our collars 'round
their pretty necks,
we give them our hearts.
They can break them
and they often do.

We maintain control;
hide our suffering.
We can't let them know
they've caused _us_ pain.
But we still shed tears
and our hearts bleed.

Art Work

The buzzing needle
penetrates my skin.
I can't see the ink,
but I feel the pain
and grip the metal

posts of the chair's back
until my fingers
cramp. The artist asks
me a question which
invades the torment

that will cloud my brain
until endorphins
kick in. He shows me
another color
and dismay requires

me to focus and
rethink the palette
I've envisioned. His
devotion to his
craft never wavers

and my trust in his
talent overrides
all my concerns. I
survive the pain and
the indecision,

but still I stagger
when, after two hours,
I stumble to the
mirror to admire
his bright creation.

I.G. Frederick

Fiction

by I.G. Frederick includes:

Cougar Conquests: Beautiful older women on the prowl and the sweet young cubs captured by their allure.

Dommemoir: A novel recounting an intense odyssey of sexual expression triumphing over sexual repression.

Eleanor & Mick: Five sizzling hot stories chronicling a journey of sexual exploration and insight.

Family Dynamics: Six sultry stories exploring sexuality in Dominant/submissive liaisons.

Fork in the Road: Three pairs of stories show how simple divergences change people's lives and relationships.

Lessons Learned: FemDom love stories about women who come to terms with their dominant sides.

Ladies in Love: Sizzling stories of Lesbian Lust

Love Hurts: Steamy stories about the dark side of love.

When Two's Not Enough: Seven sexy ménage stories

Young & Eager: Barely legal but hardly innocent teens

http://www.eroticawriter.net/

And, as Korin Dushayl:

Broken
Shattered
Playing With Dolls
Choices

http://transgressivewriter.om/

www.ingramcontent.com/pod-product-compliance
Lightning Source LLC
Chambersburg PA
CBHW061317040426
42444CB00010B/2682